SENSUAL SINS

IN

THE

TEMPLE

That's Why People Leave The Church

It's

A Read

A Workbook

And

A Journal

For Those Of You That Are New To My Writing Pattern, The Reason I Capitalize ALL My Words, Is That Words Are POWER And Every Word I Write, Speak Or Type, I Want It To Be Powerful In Its Delivery.
Normally, When You Capitalize A Word It's At The Beginning Of A Sentence When Used In A Sentence....
My Reason Is That Every Word I Write Is A Beginning To Your Understanding...

I Am Setting My *"OWN"* Standard...
AND
I AM Running With That With God...
Be It Unto You...

ACNOWLEDGEMENT

I Would Like To Thank My Lord And Savior
Jesus Christ
For All That God Has Given Me
I Recognize That The Lord Gave Me This Gift
Which Allows Me To Share With Everyone
That Participates In The Reading Of The
Literary Material That I Produce Through
The Commission Of God

Thank You Lord God
I Will Forever Be Grateful
For Your Trust In Me
Pamela Denise Brown

Copyright © 2017

Pamela Denise Brown.
All rights reserved. No part of this book may be used or reproduced by any means, graphic, electronic, or mechanical, including photocopying, recording, taping or by any information storage retrieval system without the written permission of the publisher except in the case of brief quotations embodied in critical articles and reviews.

Books Speak For You books may be ordered through booksellers or by contacting:
Books Speak For You Educational Publishing
Booksspeakforyou.com
1-800-757-0598
The views expressed in this work are solely those of the author.
Any illustration provided by iStock and such images are being used for illustrative purposes.
Certain stock imagery © iStock.
ISBN: 978-1-64050-312-0

Library Of Congress PCN Number: 2017918404

Printed in the United States Of America

Introduction To Four Reads

This Is An Introduction To All 4 Books In The 4 Book Release... That Was Suppose To Occur On My Birthday, Which Was 12/19/2017. I However, Delayed It And Decided To Release The Books On 12/25/2017 The Day Christ's Birth Is Memorialized And Celebrated.

God Poured These Books Into My Spirit And I Wrote Them Until They Were Completed. It Is My Hope That You Purchase All Four (4) Books, Because They Follow Each Other In A Spiritual Reveal And Climb.

I'm Actually Getting Ready To Write "Sensual Sins In The Temple – That's Why People Leave The Church" Right Now At This VERY Moment.
It's Sunday, December 10, 2017, Nine Days Before My Birthday AND The Release Of These 4 Books.

Guess What Guys, I Still Have To Edit "Grab A Hold Of Yourself" AND "High Treason In The Garden The Conspiracy Against Your Flesh"...
Not To Mention Write The Last Book "How To Live A Skillful Life – The Shift"...

I Know It Sounds Incomprehensible, But Just Like The Penmen That Wrote The Bible, I AM NOT The Writer, The Spirit Of God Is Using My Vessel... Hence ALL Things Are Possible With God And That's What I Represent... "All Things Are Possible"...

NOW... About The Books, They Are In Order Of A Pattern For Success, In The Natural AND In The Spirit.

1. "Grab A Hold Of Yourself".

At Some Point, You Have To Grab A Hold Of Yourself. This Is Important, Because You Cannot Be Successful, Productive Or Advance In Christ If You Have No Self Control, There Are Just Some Things You Just Can't Do Anymore. There Comes A Time In Everybody's Life When You Really Just Have To Face Exactly Who You Are, Who You're Not And Who You Really Want To Be. You Can Not Move Forward In Life Or In Christ And Never Confront Yourself, It's Just Not Possible. Your Life Is Going To Run Into A Wall At Some Point And You Will Begin To Ask Questions Regarding What's Going On In Your Life And More Importantly, What's Not Going On.

Trust Me, When You Really Desire To Live Holy, The Word Of God In You Will Start Correcting You…

God's Word Is SURE…

The Bible Says… Psalm 119:11 (KJV)

[11] Thy word have I hid in mine heart, that I might not sin against thee.

Believe Me, I Know…

You Will Eventually Be Called To Your Created, Corrected Self. (It's Marvelous) AND The Journey Is Real!!!

2. "High Treason In The Garden, The Conspiracy Against Your Flesh".

God Wants You To Know, Just Like In The Garden, The Devil Is Still Conspiring And Trying To Kill And Destroy You. There Is A Conspiracy Against Your Flesh, With Your Flesh!!!

There Is A Conspiracy Against Your Create With Who You Were Created To Be, Because There Is Still A Conspiracy Against God.

God Said, In The Beginning Was The Word And The Word Was GOD And The Word Was With God...
AND
In Matthew, God's Word Was Made Flesh...

The Devil Is Coming Against The Word "Materialized" As Flesh, Which Is YOU And The Word Made Flesh, Which Is "God In YOU".

This Read Is Powerful In Its Absolute Ability To Inform And Rescue You.
The Bible Says, We Perish For Lack Of Knowledge, Well,
"Here Comes The Light!!!".

3. "Sensual Sins In The Temple"- "That's Why People Leave The Church".

Now This Book Speaks For Itself...
I Can't Make This Stuff Up.
This Right Here Is A Must, Must, Must Read For EVERY Women.
This Book Will Definitely Open The Eyes Of Every Reader That Reads It.
The Bible Says That Even The Elite Shall Be Fooled,
But Don't Worry, God Sent Help...
Women, This Is For You.
Sometimes Your Desires Will Manifest Itself In A Way That's "Foreign" To You And That's Why Gods Word Says To Cast Down Every Imagination...
Imagination Is Powerful And Before I Look At The Word Imagination, I Want To Give You "Foreign"... Foreign Is Something That Is "Strange" AND "Unfamiliar, Unknown, Unheard Of And Perhaps Alien".

LETS LOOK AT The Definition Of Imagination:
Imagination, the faculty or action of forming new ideas, or images or concepts of external objects not present to the senses.

LOOK: This Part Of The Definition Is POWERFUL And The Delivery Of It Is Sure:

IT SAYS: Images Or "Concepts" Of External Objects NOT Present To The Senses...
(In Other Words In Connection With This Book, I'll Line This Definition Up And Say, Someone Can Imagine Doing Something To You And Because Of Your Desire, It Can Be Manifested)...
WORDS Are "Accurate" In Them AND Words Are Powerful...
AND When You Understand Them In Your Accepted Intellect, They Will Forcefully Perform For You...

LOOK AT THIS DEFINITION: Imagination Is Also **Creative Power,** fancy vision,
the *ability of the mind to be creative or resourceful*.

I Can't Make This Stuff Up Yall...

Imagination Is The Ability To Be "Creative" OR "Resourceful" AND *Resourceful Is Having The Ability To Find Quick And Clever Ways To Overcome Difficulties*.

It Means To Be "Inventive", Ingenious AND "Creative"...

COME ON IN THIS ROOM AND Get Rescued From Yourself...
In Other Words, Your Spirit In A LIE In Worship Is Finding Quick And Clever Ways To Overcome The

***Difficulties You Face As You Worship And Desire To Be Wanted, Loved And Needed*…**

Why, Because You **Forgot** That You Were Supposed To Enter Into His Courts With Thanksgiving
And
His Gates With Praise!!!

Psalm 100:4 King James Version
[4] Enter into his gates with thanksgiving, and into his courts with praise: be thankful unto him, and bless his name.
This Book Is A Must Read And That's Why People Leave The Church, Because Of Sensual Sins In The Temple, Manifested In The Flesh…
The "Temple" Of Course Being YOU!!!

Here's A Thought:
The Mind In Its Imaginative Form Can Only Be Resourceful In Its Ability To Deliver…
Pamela Denise Brown

This Book Opens The Eye Of What Desire Can Render In An Innocent Not Talked About Subtle, Sneaky, Deceptive, Deceiving, Unwarranted Way…When "Imagination" Is The Culprit!!!
Deliverance, However IS IN THE HOUSE!!!

The Fourth Book
4. "How To Live A Skillful Life - The Shift".
Here Comes Instructional Healing And Deliverance From The Lie You Tell Yourself To The Lie You Live...
You CAN NOT Be Successful In Life Without RULES!!!
That's Why We Stop At The Red Light AND Go Through The Green...
The Rule For The Red Light Means To STOP...
If We Ignore The Red Light Rule, We'll All Crash Into Each Other...
So You See, Rules Are Essential To Being Successful In Life AND Being "SAFE"...
Don't Worry, God's Got It All Covered In His Word...
Proverbs: 11 Says In Verse 14, **[14] Where no counsel is, the people fall:**

This Is All For YOU!!!
You Can Make It!!!
AND
You Will Make It!!!

Don't Be Confused, God Wants All Of Us To Be Successful At Life.
There Is However, A Paradigm Set Before Us In Christ That Is Often Ignored Or Not Taught, This Book Will "Highlight" The Paradigm.

Here's Something To Think About, The Mysteries Of Godliness Are Revealed As They Are Searched Out And The

Search Comes With Your Heart's Desire To Live Right And Read God's Word.

I Must Tell You That That Scripture, Seek Ye First The Kingdom Of Heaven And It's Righteousness And All These Things Shall Be Added Is True...
God's Word Is True. God Adds Certain Things To You After You Seek Righteousness. One Of The Things God Ads Is Your Ability To Conquer Sin. Just Ask Jesus...
 Paul Said,
[15] What then? shall we sin, because we are not under the law, but under grace? God forbid.
[16] Know ye not, that to whom ye yield yourselves servants to obey, his servants ye are to whom ye obey; whether of sin unto death, or of obedience unto righteousness?

There Comes A Time When We Must Walk Holy.
Hebrews 6:1-6(KJV) 6 Therefore leaving the principles of the doctrine of Christ, let us go on unto perfection; not laying again the foundation of repentance from dead works, and of faith toward God,

God Has Given Us Everything We Need.
I Guarantee You, After Reading These Books, You'll Be Sitting At The Feet Of The Lord In The Spirit, Grateful AND Thankful.

Sensual Sins In The Temple

That's Why People Leave The Church

Is A Nonfiction Read

The Book Is Broken Up Into Five Parts
The Story
The Truth
The Purpose Of This Book
Scriptures
AND
Words To Define

Before I Get Into The Read, I First Want To Explain To You What "Sensual" Is And As I "OPEN" You Up To Sensual, I'll Reveal It As Sin In Your Temple While Your Worshipping In A "Temple" (Building)...
Then I'll Explain Why The Battle Goes On, Because Of The Two Temples You Worship In...

Now The Word Sensual Means Of Or Arousing Gratification Of The Senses And Physical Especially Sexual Pleasure...
Synonyms To Describe "Sensual" Are, Physical, Carnal, Bodily, Fleshly, **Hedonistic, Sybaritic, Voluptuary** And I'll Use Seductive.

The Antonyms For This Word Are Spiritual And Passionless.

During The Read, You Will "Understand" Why Your Want In Worship Opposite To God, NEVER Renders To You What You Want.

For One The "Worship" Is Not In Truth.
It Is Passionless, Which Is Unemotional, Cold Blooded, Unfeeling, Impassive, Unloving And It Uses You, Because Your Worship Is A Lie.

You Must "Keep" In MIND, Spiritual Is Relating To Or Affecting The Human Spirit Or Soul As OPPOSED To Material Or Physical Things.

STOP For A Second... The Key Word Right Here, Is **OPPOSED**, Which Means *EAGER To "PREVENT"*, OR *Put An END To*:....
It's Disagreeing With What God Wants For You...

Lord Have Mercy...

NOW LETS GET BACK TO THE WORD Sensual..., Which Again Means Of Or Arousing Gratification Of The Senses and Physical, Especially Sexual Pleasure Described Also As **Hedonistic, Sybaritic And Voluptuary...**

The Synonyms For This Is...AND These Are VERY Important To The Relationship Of This Read...
The Spiritual Sin In Your Temple Invites The Practice Of This By Your Desire, Your Wants And Everything Opposite Of True Worship...
They're Nonmaterial, Psychological, Transcendent, "Mystic", Intangible AND Mental...

Now The Word **"Hedonistic"** Means **"Engaged In The "PURSUIT" Of Pleasure Sensually Self Indulgent.**

Sybaritic, However Means **FOND Of Sensuous "Luxury" OR "Pleasure"...**
AND
Voluptuary, Means **A Person DEVOTED To Sensual Pleasure...**

This Is So Powerful, Because Your Spirit Can Be In The "Pursuit" Of Something You Don't Quite Understand And Once That Pursuit Is Activated And Becomes Devoted To The Gratification Of It You Can Become FOND Of What It Served You In An Innocent Way...
Why, Because It's All "Spiritual", But OPPOSITE To The Truth Of Who God Is And That's Why The Word Said To Worship God In "Spirit" And In Truth...

The Truth, Being The Word Of God And NOT Attaching Anything To It In Our Isolated Worship...

Because, Again And I Must Reiterate This Over And Over, Sensual Is Of Or Arousing Gratification Of The Senses AND Physical...

You Have Aroused... The Sense Of What Sensual Is In Your Worship As You Worshipped In Your NEED, WANT And DESIRE...

Listen,
 I'm Going To Give You One More Word Before I Get Into The Story And That Word Is Sense...

Sense: A Faculty By Which The Body Perceives An External Stimulus; One Of The Faculties Of Sight, Smell, Hearing, Taste AND **Touch**...

This Book Is About Sensual Sins In The Temple AND The Sense Of Touch Spiritually....

As Paradox As This May Sound, It Nevertheless Is Proved... **I AM... "Proof"'**

The Scripture Below References What Was Witnessed In Chapter 5 Of The Book Of Acts And Likewise Is Relevance To The Witnessing Of What We Witness As Children Of God...

God Is The Same God He Has Always Been And Life Reflects That.

Life Procreates Itself Through Us In Life...

Acts 5:32 King James Version
[32] And we are his witnesses of these things; and so is also the Holy Ghost, whom God hath given to them that obey him.

UNDERSTANDING...

I Need You To "Understand" How Your Mind Serves You Pleasure In An Unorthodox Way And If You Don't "Grab A Hold" Of Yourself, It Will Keep Grabbing A Hold Of You.

The Control Is Gained After You Master The "Conception" And That "Mastery" Is Only Gained By "Practice", Which Sometimes Can Only Be Gained By "Participation"...

It's Scientific...

The Study Of Such Renders You Knowledge OR In Some Cases "How To" AND How To "NOT".
Everything We Go Through Is To Help Others And When You Ask God To Use You, Brace Yourself, Because The Ride, The Walk, The Discovery And The Journey Will Be Nothing Like You Expect.

"Sensual Sins In The Temple" Is A "Secret" YOU Keep With Yourself, But God Said In Mark 4:22 King James Version [22] For there is nothing hid, which shall not be manifested; neither was anything kept secret, but that it should come abroad.
AND In Luke It Says: Luke 8:17 King James Version [17] For nothing is secret, that shall not be made manifest; neither anything hid, that shall not be known and come abroad.

Wait A Minute... Here Comes Matthew To Help: AND Deliver Us From Our Fear...

Matthew 10:26 King James Version **26 Fear Them NOT Therefore**: For There Is Nothing Covered, That Shall Not Be Revealed; And Hid, That Shall Not Be Known.

NOW I Will Give You "Temple" Defined Two (2) Ways AND Then We'll Get Into The Book…

The First Definition Will Come From The Merriam Dictionary, It Tells Us That A "Temple" Is A "Building" "Devoted" To The Worship, Or "Regarded" As The Dwelling Place, Of A God Or Gods Or Other Objects Of Religious Reverence…
House Of God…

The Word TEMPLE Is Also Explained Biblically Like This,

In John 2:19 Jesus Answered And Said Unto Them, Destroy This Temple, And In Three Days I Will Raise It Up.

1 Corinthians 6:19 Says… What? Know Ye NOT That Your Body Is The Temple Of The Holy Ghost **Which Is IN YOU**, Which Ye Have Of God, And **Ye Are NOT Your Own?**

When You Worship Spirit,

Spirit Worship's Spirit…

AND If You're Not In The Right Spirit Of Your Worship To God, You Worship In That Spirit And Not To God…

That's Why The Word Says,

John 4:24 King James Version
[24] God Is A Spirit: And They That Worship Him Must Worship Him In Spirit And In Truth.

FIRST OF ALL, And You Can Believe It Or NOT…
When You Come In God's House With The "Intent" To "WORSHIP" In What We Call The "Temple" Building, Thinking About Your Desires Or "Concentrating" On Anything Other Than God, Like The Fact That You're Lonely In A Way That Doesn't Allow God To Be Comfort For You, You Open Yourself Up To A Spirit That's Not Truth And You Therefore Allow Yourself To Be Used By A Force That Is Foreign And Unrecognizable To You, Because You Are Spiritually Revealed In That Spirit.

Let's Face It…
Some Of Us Set Ourselves Up To Be "Used", Because We REALLY Don't Understand What It Means To Worship God In Spirit And In Truth…

Life Is REAL And Like I Said Earlier,
The TRUTH Is BIGGER Than Reality…

Now That That's Done,
LET'S GET INTO THIS BOOK

Enjoy The Read!!!

The Invitation:

Patricia Had Just Got Home. As She Sat Down On The Steps In Her Mother's House, The Phone Rang. It Was Her First Love, Who She Had Not Seen In A Long While, He Was Now A Pastor And When Patricia Picked Up The Phone And Heard His Voice, She Was Excited, Eager And Surprised.

Patricia Had Not Heard From Him In A While, But Every Time He Called Her, No Matter Where She Was Or What She Was Doing, She Would Stop Doing It.

Patricia's Life Would Come To A Halt, Until What Her Friend Wanted From Her, Revealed Itself. It Was Strange, But He Had The Ability To Stop Anything That Was Going On In Her Life From Continuing.

The Call...He Was Calling To Inform Patricia That God Had Sent Him To Get Her To Be A Part Of His Ministry. She Was Intrigued And Her Love For Him Moved Her And She Accepted The Invitation.

I Want To Talk To You, He Said In A Charismatic Voice. Let's Meet.
Excited, Patricia Agreed To Meet Her Friend, Who Was A Pastor.
He Picked Her Up And Brought Her Back To His Office. It Was Then That He Explained His Ministry And Asked If She Would Help Him. He Informed Her That God Wanted The Best Out Of Her Life And God Had Sent Him To Get Her. He Told Her That He Had Been To The Mountain (I Imagine, This Was The Mountain Of God) And He Told Her That God Sent Him Back Down To Get His Body.

Whatever That Meant...

Patricia At That Point, Decided In Her Mind That She Would Gain Back The Love That Had Ended Suddenly From Her Youth...

Game On...

The Pastor, Who Was Her First Love Had No Idea, About The Thoughts That Ran Through Her Mind And Whatever He Asked...
Inwardly, She Was Prepared To Do...

They Started Meeting Up At His Office And She Helped Him With Office Work.

She Also Began To Work In The Church. Her Life Progressed And Things Changed. God Began To Open Doors For Patricia And She Began To Be Extremely Blessed Financially.
Things Were Going Good. The Two Of Them Started Getting Closer And Eventually Started Sharing Meals.

THE FIRST ENCOUNTER...
Patricia Is At The Restaurant Having Dinner With Her Friend, Enjoying His Company In A Relaxed Atmosphere. It's A Hot Summer Night, She's Feeling Confident About How She Looks And In The Back Of Her Mind, She Is Hoping That The Love Of Her Life Is "Feeling Her"... The Dinner Is Over And He Stands By Her Chair And Waits For Her To Get Up...
Always The Perfect Gentleman...
They Head To The Car And Get In. As They're Driving Down The Street, She Begins To Have This Inner Body

Experience As If She's Being Caressed And Fondled. Then As She Sits There In The Car, Not Knowing What To Do Or Say, She Closes Her Eyes In Total Shock And Astonishment As She Secretly Calls On God For Rescue.

What Is This, She Says Several Times To Herself, Squirming In The Seat Of The Car Trying To Escape The Feeling Of Someone Oscillating Up And Down Her Thighs...

What Is This...

The Rush From The Encounter Was So Sudden And Rapid. The Experience Almost Caused Her To Lose Consciousness In Its Delivery.

The Feeling Of Someone Actually Having Intercourse Uninvited, Unscheduled And Unannounced Wore Her Down And As The Rush Subsided, Patricia Sat There Staring Out The Window Trying To Figure Out What Was Happening.

Who Was Responsible For This, She Thought And What Force Of Nature Authored It.

There Were So Many Emotions Running Through Patricia's Mind. She Was Frightened, Astonished AND Blank All At The Same.

Hoping She Could Disappear During The Encounter, Her Friend Noticing Her Uncontrollable Squirming, Leg Crossing And Silent Moan... Said, Just Hold On, It's Going To Be Ok...

Hold On It's Going To Be Ok...

Patricia's Like What Do You Mean, It's Going To Be Ok.

Patricia Couldn't Understand Why He Would Be Saying That...
How Could He Know What Was Going On...
Although, It Was Obvious That Patricia Was Under Some Sort Of Attack, Patricia Secretly Didn't Want To Expose Herself To Him, Nor Did She Want Him To Discover The Siege.

This Was More Than Patricia Could Bare And As She Continued To Squirm And Almost Lose Her Natural Mind, The Strokes Kept Coming And Each Stroke In Touch Drove Her Mad.
She Squirmed And Squirmed, Wishing It Would End, But It Only Escalated...

The Experience Was Something She Could Never Imagine...

What In God's Name Is This...
She Wasn't Participating...
How Could She...
It Just Took Over And Had Its Way With Her...
The Force Of The Encounter Was Intense, Foreign And Unfamiliar.

It Reared It's Sensual, Sexual, Seductive Head And Patricia Found Herself "Captured" In The Moment...

While Sitting In The Seat Squirming, Practically Out Of Breath From The Rush, Patricia Saw Her Friend Watching In Her Peripheral Vision, Still Driving And The Only Thing She Could Remember Him Saying Was,
It's Going To Be Alright.

Are You Ok, He Said Again…
Patricia Sat There Not Knowing What To Do.
The Movement All Over Her Body Required Attention And She Didn't Know How To Give It…
How Could She…
It's Origin Was Not Revealed Nor Was It Invited…

Are You Ok, Her Friend Said Again.

From The Tone Of His Concerned Voice At This Point,
It Sounded As If He Was Taking Ownership.

Patricia Wanted Answers. Totally Embarrassed And Consumed, Still In Denial And Unbelief That Any One Could Actually Be Doing This To Her, Patricia Continued In The Conversation With No Clue As To What He Was Talking About Or What Was Going On. Subdued By The Encounter, She Concentrated On Catching Her Breath, Which She Was Losing With Every Stroke That Touched Her Body.

The Moisture She Felt Was Real, So The Encounter Was With Someone Or Something, Patricia Just Didn't Know Who OR What.

The Rest Of The Ride Was In Silence As Patricia Scaled Down In Her Anxiety After The Climax.

Apparently, He Didn't Know What To Say. Still Shocked, Patricia Looked At Him With Innocent Eyes As She Tried To Figure Out Without Exposing Her Embarrassment What Had Just Occurred, But She Couldn't.

Anxiety Sat In…

She Was Puzzled, Perplexed And Confused.
She Had Never Experienced Anything Like This In Her Life. The Feeling That Something Foreign Took Over Her Body, Caressed And Literally Had Intercourse With Her Without Her Permission Was More Than She Could Bear And She Sat There Quietly, Still Squirming.

As They Continued To Drive, She Didn't Know If He Was Watching Her Out Of Amusement Or Concern.

Did He Orchestrate This?
She Asked Herself Over And Over.
All Kinds Of Scenarios Ran Through Her Head.

WAS THIS HIM...
Did He Do This???

If It Was Him, She Wondered Was He Giving Himself A Pat On The Back For His Successful Ability To Go Into Her And Have Her Uncontrollably Engage In Intercourse...

Was This Going On In His Mind She Thought...

What Is Going On...

Whatever It Was, She Felt Like She Had Been Touched For The First Time And There Was NO BODY...
I Mean No "Body"...
No "Penis"...
There Was Nothing Tangible Attached To This Encounter...
And The One Question That Would Not Leave Her Mind Was,
HOW...
How Could This Happen...

She Didn't Lay Down...
She Wasn't Asked...
There Was No Foreplay...
She Never Opened Her Legs...

HOW COULD THIS HAPPEN...
They Pulled Up In Front OF Patricia's Mother's House And He Softly Asked Her Did She Enjoy Herself...
Still Captured By The Encounter, Patricia Nods Her Head And Suddenly Reaches For The Door To Escape.
At This Point Patricia Wanted To Be Anywhere But In The Car.
The Car Had Become A Cell...
She Was Boxed In And Had No Where To Go...
So As She Gasped For Breath Again, She Finally Was Able To Gain What Little Control She Had Over Her Body And Reach For The Door, Using The Handle As A Crutch To Pull Herself Out.
Once She Got Out, Sucking The Air In,
She Quickly Walked A Few Steps To Her Mother's House, Barely Looking Back To Waive Goodbye.

Patricia's Focus And Only Aim Was On Getting Inside The House...
Wondering If She Should Look Back Or Smile To Indicate That The Night Was Good, She Instead Walked Straight To The Door.

She Didn't Know What To Do...

Still Embarrassed, She Didn't Know If He Really Knew What Was Going On, So She Hurried And Kept Walking To Her Mothers Door.

I'll Call You Later She Said, In A Haste After She Was Safe On Her Mother's Porch.

Trying To Get Into The House, Patricia Could Not Chance Another Encounter By Looking Back, Because At This Point, She Thought The Culprit Was Whatever Was In The Car.

All Of A Sudden, She Pushed Her Way Into The House As If The House Rescued Her.

Patricia Is Now Inside Her Mother's Door...
Holding On To The Wall Inside Still Consumed By A Feeling Of Intercourse, She Begins To Ask Herself Questions...

After All, Who Else Would She Ask...
Trying To Explain This Would Just Sound Crazy... It Was Crazy...

Patricia Goes To Sit Down And Touch Herself.
Discovering The Moisture In Her Underwear From The Encounter, She Rushes Upstairs To Investigate And Shower.
Patricia Had Been Celibate Now For About 4 Years At The Time Of The Encounter, This Was 7 Years Ago To Date.

After Patricia Got Upstairs, She Started Having Conversations With Herself Asking The Same Questions Over And Over Again...

Did He Do That???

Does He Have The Capability To Do That???

Is He Possessed???

Did He Possess Me???

Is This Real???

Am I Dreaming Or Imagining This???

What Just Happened???

Is He Practicing Witchcraft???

Did Someone Put Something In My Water???

Did I Eat Something???

Was There A Hex Put On Me???

What THE HELL Happened???

Patricia Sat There Mentally Scrambling Asking Herself All Sorts Of Questions...
This Was Puzzling And The Fact That He Sat There During The Whole Ordeal, Disturbed Her Even More..

Perhaps He Wasn't The Culprit...
Perhaps He Was,..
Patricia Had No Answers, So She Just Basically Carried On As If It Didn't Happen.

Confession Time...
Now Before I Go On, I Have To Confess And Come Out Of Character.

I Can Not Continue To Write This Book In Second Person Mode, Because In Order For Deliverance To Occur, There Must Be Exposure.

I Have To KEEP IT REAL.

This Book Is Not About Patricia, This Book Is About Me...
Everything I'm Writing In This Book Actually Happened To Me Why I Was In Church And It's One Of The Many Reason's I Left...
Hence, "Sensual Sins In The Temple... That's Why People Leave The Church"...

Now That That's Out The Way, Let's Keep Moving...

I'm Going To Go Back To The Encounter Before I Move Forward.
I Didn't Know How To Feel.

I Was Blown Away.

There Had Been An Invasion...
An Encounter...
Intercourse Had Occurred And I Was Like **What The Heck Is This**...
There Wasn't A Discussion Or Anything.

I Think My Friend Was Stunned That I Didn't Really Understand What Happened And The Reason Why I Can Say That Now Out Of Character, Is Because I Believe He Knew What I Was Going Through...

You'll See As The Story Continues To Unfold.

Deliverance Only Comes With Exposure...
Maybe, I Needed To Be Delivered From My Secret Thoughts Toward Him!!!

The Bible Says: For Though We Walk In The Flesh, We Do Not War After The Flesh:

We Must Keep In Mind, The War We Fight Is Spiritual...
And
Sometimes When We're In A "Battle" AND We're Warring, We Don't Think About Using Our Sword To Defend Us.
(Side Bar – Some Things Are Spiritual Battles AND Some Things Are Spiritual "Consequences")

Back To The Book: I Know I Wasn't Thinking About A "Spiritual Sword" During This Encounter, I Was 100% Focused On Where It Was Coming From And Why It Was Occurring.

Remember, I Had Just Went Back To Church, So The Only Thing I Was Doing Was "Churchin".

I Never Included A Relationship With God With Going To Church, I Don't Remember If That Was Even Taught To Me...
I Mean, I Was Raised To Love Jesus And All, Because Of Who He Was.
Regardless Of Troubles, Loving Jesus Was Just That, "Loving Jesus"...
And In Retrospect, I Don't Believe I Really Even Knew What It Meant To Love Jesus Really, Because I've Learned Now That To Love Jesus Means To Keep The Commandments.

God Is Bringing Hidden Things Into The Light And That's The ONLY Purpose For This Book, Like I Said Before, In Order For Deliverance To Take Place, There Has To Be Exposure.

The Bible Says In 2nd Corinthians 10:4

^{4}(For the weapons of our warfare are not carnal, but mighty through God to the pulling down of strong holds;)
^{5} **Casting down imaginations**, and every high thing that exalteth itself against the knowledge of God, **and bringing into captivity every thought to the obedience of Christ;**
(I'm Going To Tap Into This Scripture Briefly And Revisit It At The End Of The Book To Bring The Sensual Sin That's Committed Sometimes Unaware And Innocently, Into A Visionary Reveal)

1 Corinthians 4:5 King James Version Says,
^{5} Therefore judge nothing before the time, until the Lord come, who both will bring to light the hidden things of darkness, and will make manifest the counsels of the hearts: and then shall every man have praise of God.

LET US KEEP WALKING...

Thank God That's Over...
What Was That I Thought.
Did He Do That...
Can Somebody Really Possess The Ability To Have Intercourse With Someone Without Having Sex...
Can Someone Really Have Complete Control Over Someone...
Can Someone Really Touch Someone Without Laying A Finger On Them...

Can You Really Be Penetrated Without A Penis...

HOW IS THIS POSSIBLE???

I Kept This Experience A Secret...
Later On I Found Out That There's A Name Attached To Acts That You Know About, But You're Not Suppose To Talk About...

I'll Whisper It...

It's "Esoteric"

This Was Esoteric In A Sense...

It Was Rarefied...
Defined As Being Distant From The Lives And Concerns Of "Ordinary" People...
Exclusive
AND Select.
Bringing Me Right Back To Esoteric...

Which Means, *"Intended For Or Likely To Be Understood By Only A Small Number Of People With Specialized Knowledge Or Interest...*
And Guess What... I Didn't Know ANYONE Who Had An Interest In This...

I Have To Tell You, Just Writing About This And Understanding The Spiritual Battles And Consequences That Go On Is Incomprehensible...
You Are In Battles You Don't Even Understand, Fights You Didn't Start...

AND What's Even More Incomprehensible Is You Don't Have A Choice But To Battle, Which Can Be Tiring...

Lord Have Mercy Up In Here, I Have Been Through Hell...

I Imagine Just To Side Bar A Little, God Allowed This To Happen, To Get Me Where He Needed Me And That's Probably Why I'm Writing This Book, To Help You Get To Where Your Supposed To Be Too...

Sit In Your Seat!!!

Now Back To The Story...

When I Was Going Through The First Experience/Encounter, I Kept It A Secret, That Was Until I Mastered The Experience And Started To Like It...

Now I Know You Thought This Would Go Another Way, But Just Hold On, We're Still Walking...

So Hush!!!

I'm Keeping It Real...

Exposing Myself For Your Deliverance AND The Continuance Of Mine!!!

Anyway, I Wanted To Know Was Anyone Else Experiencing This In The Church Or Anywhere On Earth... What Is Going On, I Thought.

THE QUEST...

I Started To Ask Around On The Down Low, Having Hypothetical Conversations... Trying To Get Answers From People, Without Sounding Crazy...

So Since I Couldn't Help But To Sound Crazy, I Just Let It Go....

Unable To Look This Person In The Face After The Encounter, I Ignored Him As Long As I Could, After All, He Came Back To Get Me To Help In The Ministry...

A Few Days Went By...

He Called...

I Answered...

AND

He Came...

SERVITUDE...

I Began Serving In The Church...
Repentance Is Taking Place And Through It All, I Was Still Trying To Figure Out What Happened.

What Happened...

Ok, I'm Going To Ignore This An Continue On In The Ministry, After All It's Working For Me And Now, I'm Being Introduced To The Laws Of God.

Here Comes Order In My Life.
I've Really Been Trying To Live Holy...
I Rededicated My Life To God And My Heart And Intentions Were Pure...
I Paid My Tithes And Gave My Offerings Cheerfully..
Church Was Getting So Good, I Invited My Friends, And Cousin To Attend The Services...
There Was Something Off However And I Could Not Put My Hand On It.
I Was Growing And Presented My Body As A Living Sacrifice, I Thought, But I Was Still Entertaining The Thoughts Of Seducing The Pastor...
I Began To Give More Time...
More Money And Whenever There Was An Opportunity For Me To Accompany The Ministry On An Outing, I Was There Encouraging The Pastor And Supporting His Endeavors.

This Went On For Years And The Encounters Increased And Worsened...

I Was Under A Spiritual Attack Constantly And I Could Not Track Or Trace The Origin Of It...

I Worshipped, I Participated, I Gave, I Came, I Helped, I Stayed...

AND Again,

I Participated...
I Gave...
I Came..
I Helped...
I Stayed...
And I Was Available Whenever There Was A Need...

I Thought I Separated My Worship And Desire, But Somehow They Were Still Parallel, One To The Other And The Spirit World Served Me In What Was A Whirlwind Of Witchcraft Practices That I Could Not Pin Point...

Every Time I Took My Anointed Self In The Church, Worshipping What I Thought Was God In The Spirit Of My Temple, I Was Afterward Rushed And Subdued By A Force That I Did Not Recognize...
I Cried...
I Questioned It...
I Sought Help...
I Asked Questions...
I Investigated...

The Snow Fell And The Floor Rumbled...

AND I Still Worshipped God With Lust, Desire, Want And Seduction On My Mind Every Time I Was In The

Presence Of The Pastor, Who Was A Single Man And The Love Of My Life, Hand Picked And Chosen By God...

I Was Very Good At Hiding This Outwardly, Because I Considered Myself A "Professional"...
lol
Whatever That Meant...
AND I Am Laughing At Myself...
Anyway Guys, God Is Good To Us And
I Believe He Knew About My Hidden Desire And Used That Against Me, Secretly, "Prostituting" His Gifts For Gain...

Hold On!!! I Know That Sounds Disrespectful And Out Of Reach, But The "Truth" Will Set You Free And Me Telling You The Truth Will Keep ME Free..

You Should Know That There Are Several Ministers In The Pulpit Prostituting Their Gifts...
Some Don't Know It And Practice "Without" The Knowledge And Some Do Know It And Practice "With" The Knowledge...

SIDE BAR...
(My Mother Was A Usher, Then A Sunday School Teacher, Then A Missionary That Traveled The World, Then A Evangelist, Then A Minister, Then She Had A Gospel Radio Show, Then A Assistant Pastor Then A Pastor So Let Me Be Clear, I Sat In Plenty Of Backrooms During Conventions, Revivals And Anniversary Celebrations And Some Of The Conversations The Men Where Having As Pastor's Talking About How They Play Women Where Not Of God AND Guess What, **THEY ALL BLAMED THE WOMEN** For Putting Herself As They Say "Out There Like That")

So Please... Stop Living In Denial, Sensual Sins In The Temple Is Real AND That's Why People Leave The Church... It's True...

Here Is A Question:

What Is Your "Intent" When You Go To Church???

NOW LET'S MOVE ON, I Need You To "SEE" This So You Won't Get "Trapped"...

First We Need To Be Clear What Prostitution Is...
Not To Confuse The "Complete" Definition About Some Women Selling Her Body On The Street...
Let Me **DEFINE** Prostitute For You;
One Of The Definitions For Prostitute Is: *Offer Someone For Sexual Activity In Exchange For Payment...* **The** *Second* **Definition** *HOWEVER, Is* **To Put ONSELF Or One's TALENTS To An Unworthy Or CORRUPT Use Or PURPOSE For The Sake Of PERSONAL Or Financial Gain...**

All I Wanted To Do Was Seduce Him, (At Least That's What I Thought) And That Thought Ran Rapid And At The Forefront Of My Mind Every Time I Saw Him, It Was Game On...

He Was Prostituting His Gifts And I Thought I Was Gaining... Only To Be Disappointed, Because **God Don't Bless NO MESS!!!**
In Other Words, His Purpose AND Mines Towards Each Other Was Not *Totally* Holy, We Both Was Using Each Other...
I'm Just Women Enough To Admit It...

I Started Off "Victim" And Them Became "Culprit"...

Don't Get Me Wrong, Moving Forward, There Were Times I Wanted Nothing To Do With Him At All, They Eventually Subsided And I Was "Always" Placed Right Back Where I Started... In My Lust And Desire.

What Was Puzzling To Me, Then And NOW, Is That My Servitude To God Was Real...

AND

My Intentions Where To Please God And Still Are.

I Thought, That Pleasing Him, Would Be To Please God, But What I Didn't Understand Is That, *Because I "Worshipped" In My Temple, In The "Temple" With My Mind Not Totally In Alignment With The Almighty, I Opened Myself Up For Misconception And Delusion.*

What's Funny And "Clear" To Me Now Is That The People On The Pulpit Play A Role In This Too...

The Spirit Of A Person Is Tried By The Spirit And When That "Spirit" Is "Revealed" And There Is A Need That Spirit Will

"Resourcefully" Find A Way To Rear It's Crafty, Clever, Claws Like A "Crouching" Tiger And Have Its Way...

There Is A Scripture In Colossians That Says, Touch Not, Taste Not, Handle Not... Not Withstanding The Meaning Of The Scripture, There Are Some Things, We Just Should Not Do...

What's Sad It That, People Really Don't Understand What It Means To Worship God In Spirit And In Truth ...

Some People Argue That Society Makes Men Without Jobs Thieves...
AND
Some Say They Should Keep Looking Until They Find Legitimate Ways To Provide For Their Families...

I Argue That People That Come In The Church With The Wrong Intentions, Make Pastor's "Prostitutes"...
Why,
Because, Of Their NEEDS...
AND
Wrongful Worship...
Remember Now...
We Are Supposed To Be Worshipping God In Spirit And In Truth And When You Worship In Spirit With Something Other Than Serving God On Your Mind, You Invite Other Sprits In...

It's True Whether You Believe It Or Not...

Look At What God's Word Says In Romans...

Romans 13:4 King James Version
⁴ For He Is The Minister Of God To Thee For Good. But If Thou Do That Which Is Evil, Be Afraid; For He Beareth Not The Sword In Vain: For He Is The Minister Of God, A Revenger To Execute Wrath Upon Him That Doeth Evil.

What We Have To Remember Is That God Is Always On The Throne And Everybody Is Expected To Obey The Word Of God...

God Judges In Righteousness And For Those Of Us That Leave The Church, Because Of A Wrong That We Initiated **Or Not**, God Will Always Have The Last Say, It's Up To Us To "Honestly" Search Our Hearts And Find Out Whether Or Not We Were The Culprit Of Our Own Consequences Or Destruction...

God's Word Is Sure And We Can Be Confident That It Will Render The "Perfect" Verdict...

LOOK At What Jeremiah Says...
Jeremiah 23-25 King James Version
23 Woe Be Unto The Pastors That Destroy And Scatter The Sheep Of My Pasture! Saith The Lord.
² Therefore Thus Saith The Lord God Of Israel Against The Pastors That Feed My People; Ye Have Scattered My Flock, And Driven Them Away, And Have Not Visited Them: Behold, I Will Visit Upon You The Evil Of Your Doings, Saith The Lord.
³ And I Will Gather The Remnant Of My Flock Out Of All Countries Whither I Have Driven Them, And Will Bring Them Again To Their Folds; And They Shall Be Fruitful And Increase.

⁴ And I Will Set Up Shepherds Over Them Which Shall Feed Them: And They Shall Fear No More, Nor Be Dismayed, Neither Shall They Be Lacking, Saith The LORD.

It's Time To Get Back In Church...

But What's More Important Is That, **We Learn The Rules...** So We Don't Become "Victims" To The "Crouching Tigers"...

We Need To Know The Rules...
 So That We Don't Get Caught Up In Our Isolated Desires...

We Need To Know The Rules...
So That We'll Know How To Worship...

We Need To Know The Rules...
So That We'll Understand That The Devil Comes To Kill, To Steal And To Rob...

We Need To Know The Rules... So That When It's Offering Time, Instead Of Feeling Like We're Being Taking Advantage Of, We'll Understand That God's Word Says, **He Loves A "Cheerful" Giver** And God's Word Teaches Us NOT To Give Out Of "Necessity"...

LOOK... God's Word IS Absolute And All You Have To Do Is STUDY... Remember That Little Scripture...
We Perish For "Lack" Of Knowledge...
Well, I DON'T CARE WHAT Any Ones Says From The Pulpit To The Door...
The Bible Says, God Loveth A "Cheerful" Giver...
God Doesn't Want Us To Give Him Grudgingly OR Of Necessity...

Let's Look At Necessity Before You Read This Scripture...
I'm Going To Set YOU FREE...

Necessity Is The Quality Or State Of Being Necessary...
And Necessary Means "NEEDED"...

So In Other Words... ***God Is "Plainly" Saying NOT To Give Out Of What Is Needed...***

Now Here's The Scripture:

2 Corinthians 9:7 King James Version
[7] Every Man According As He Purposeth In His Heart, So Let Him Give; Not Grudgingly, Or Of Necessity: For God Loveth A Cheerful Giver.

Don't Get Mad, If You Give It, They'll Take It...

God Loves A Cheerful Giver, So Whatever You Give, Whether It's Your Time, Your Money Or Your Heart, Make Very Sure That You Are Giving It To God And Not Wanting Anything In Return, But To Please God...

Anything Else Is A Lie...

A Lie You Tell Yourself That Will Not Result In The Return You Expect...
Trust Me, I Know...

I'm Glad I Made It Out ***And When I Say Out,*** I Mean Out Of The "Prison" In My Mind, The Lie Of Worshiping In Spirit AND Truth With NO Attachments...

The Truth Is, I Fought Constantly In The Spirit And I NEVER Looked At Myself As The Inviting Culprit...

I Never Thought For One Moment, That It Was My Spirit That Had Orchestrated The Whole Ordeal.
(After All, I Was "Anointed". Did You Forget Gifts Come Without Repentance?)

Until TODAY, As I Am Writing This Book, It Never Dawned On Me That I Was "Playing" A Game With Myself...
A Spiritual Game That I Would Never Win, Because I Involved The Worship Of God In A Lie...

I Never Looked At What I Was Doing As Wrong...
I Never Sought To Address My Own Lust...
I Never Questioned Myself And My Desires As Something That Was Not Permissible In Church, In My Temple Or In The Temple...
AND Although, So Many Things Happened To Me That Were Intentional, My Hidden Desire Served Me A Lie And The Spirit Of Confusion, Hidden Agenda, Deceit, Deception, Usury, Fraud, Callousness, Uncaring, Misrepresentation AND Everything Opposite To God Ran Rapid And Eventually Had It's Fair Game With Me And I Left The Church Tired And Worn OUT!!!

BUT Wait...

I Learned The Game And Came Back To The Church Several Times, Playing The Game That Was Played On Me On Them AND Every Time They Thought They Had Their "Hooks" In Me, I Would Leave Them Flat Dry To Prove A Point...

This Went On For A While Until God Addressed And Confronted Me With My Sin...
Just Wait For It, God Will Show Up...

AND

God Will Judge...

Although A Lot Of Judgment Was In My Favor, I Was Responsible For My Part And God Bought It To A HALT!!!

People On Both Sides Lost A Lot, Members Left The Church (Until It Was Just One Member Left Who Accepted The Practice Of Witchcraft On Her Like It Was A Way Of Life, It Was Horrifying To Watch) , Houses Were Taken, Jobs Lost, Houses Burnt Down, Death Occurred, People Were Hospitalized And Placed In Mental Institutions...

God Judged AND I Mean He Judged...

From The Pulpit To The Door...

The Practice Of Witchcraft Ran Rapid... AND The Spirit Of Seduction Was Released To Gain...

It Was The Most Dreadful, Unnatural Thing I Have Ever Endured... BUT GOD Brought It To A End...

The End...

You See Sometimes, Sin Presents Itself And You First Start Out As The ***"Victim"*** Then All Of A Sudden, The Tables Turn As You Become The ***"Culprit"***...

Now In Becoming The *"Culprit"* Let Me Show You The *"Consequences"* Of What That Means In Gods Word Or Rather What It *Serves* YOU...

Ezekial 33: 21-20 SAYS...

[12] Therefore, thou son of man, say unto the children of thy people, *The righteousness of the righteous shall not deliver him in the day of his transgression: as for the wickedness of the wicked, he shall not fall thereby in the day that he turneth from his wickedness*; neither shall the righteous be able to live for his righteousness in the day that he sinneth.

[13] When I shall say to the righteous, that he shall surely live; if he trust to his own righteousness, and commit iniquity, *all his righteousnesses shall not be remembered*; but for his iniquity that he hath committed, he shall die for it.

[14] Again, when I say unto the wicked, Thou shalt surely die; if he turn from his sin, and do that which is lawful and right;

[15] If the wicked restore the pledge, give again that he had robbed, walk in the statutes of life, without committing iniquity; he shall surely live, he shall not die.

[16] *None of his sins that he hath committed shall be mentioned unto him: he hath done that which is lawful and right; he shall surely live.*

[17] Yet the children of thy people say, The way of the Lord is not equal: but as for them, their way is not equal.

[18] *When the righteous turneth from his righteousness, and committeth iniquity, he shall even die thereby.*

[19] But if the wicked turn from his wickedness, and do that which is lawful and right, he shall live thereby.

[20] Yet ye say, The way of the Lord is not equal. *O ye house of Israel, I will judge you every one after his ways.*

God Is NOT Playing With You...
AND
God Is Certainly NOT Playing With Me...
The Devil Is So Clever...
Your Job Is To Stay Focused And In Right Fellowship With God, Because One Wrong Move Can Take You On A Ride That You Will Beg To Get Off And In This Case, I Had To Go Through The Process And Be Taught A Lesson... **(Consequences)**

Hopefully, You Won't Have Too, Because You'll Read This Book And Understand The Importance Of True Worship...

And

Deliverance...

Deliverance Is Definitely In The House, But You First Have To Face Yourself And Face Your Wrong...

You Have To Look Yourself In The Face And See The Lie, The Deceit, The Misconception And Then The Truth...

Deliverance Can Only Come, When You Face The Truth Of The Lie That You Live And Tell Yourself Daily...

Once That Is Achieved, Deliverance Can Happen...

Thank God For Deliverance And Repentance And Thank God For The Truth...

Let's LOOK At What The Truth Is...

This Will Definitely Set You Free... LOOK!!!

The Truth

The Power Of Words Is "Powerful"
And In My Thoughts As I Worshipped In The Spirit Of What I Thought Was God, It Manifested Itself Indeed.

You See **To Worship** Means To **Treat Someone Or "Something" With Reverence And Adoration *"Appropriate To A Deity"*...**

Lord Have Mercy Up In Here...
It Also Means To Glorify, Exalt And Extol And You Can Worship In A Religious Ceremony And Give Your Worship To Another Deity, Because Of "Desire"...

Look, Deity Can Be Defined And Shown In Two Different Ways... It All Depends On Your Mind Set During The Time Of Worship...

Deity Is A **"Divine Status"**, A God Or Goddess, A Divine Being, Supreme Being, Quality ...

OR

AND This Is Key Right Here...
Or Nature

Now The Divine Status, Quality Or Nature
Can Be A "Ruler", Which In This Case Is Satan, The "Ruler" Of Darkness...
Let's Face It LUST Is By No Means LIGHT!!!

Now The Divine Status Of A Deity Worshipped, Is Manifested By A Ruler Driven By Delusions Of That Deity In Nature Of Your Worship...

And The Delusion... Is
An Idiosyncratic "Belief" OR "Impression" **That Is Firmly "MAINTAINED"** Despite Being "Contradicted" By What Is "Generally Accepted" As Reality Or Rational Argument... Some Might Say That This Is Typically A Symptom Of MENTAL Disorder...

Lord Have Mercy Up In Here...

That's Why God Said To *"Cast Down"* Every Imagination By The Pulling Down Of Strongholds...
Desire... Stronghold In The Church
Lust... Stronghold In The Church
Want... Stronghold In The Church
Loneliness... Stronghold In The Church
Neediness... Stronghold In The Church
Pitiful... Stronghold In The Church
Helplessness... Stronghold In The Church
AND Let's Be "CLEAR"

The Church Is In YOU!!!

You See, The Delusion As You Sit In Service Wanting Something That Doesn't Belong To You, Or Desiring Something In Your Worship That Does Not Line Up With God, You Know When You Imagine Laying That Man Down And Performing That Trick That Will Make Him Scream And Call Out Your Mother's Name...
Thanking Her For Having You...
You Know That Imagination...

Guess What, It Serves You
A Misconception,
A Misunderstanding,
A Misrepresentation
And
Misinterpretation Of TRUTH...
WHY...
Because YOU ARE IN ERROR...

Glory To God...
The Bible Says...
Psalm 100:4(KJV)
⁴ *Enter Into His Gates With Thanksgiving, And Into His Courts With Praise: Be Thankful Unto Him, And Bless His Name.*

CHECK MATE: When You Come In With Anything Else, You Become A Target Of Misconception And Misinterpretation, Because You Open Yourself Up To A Spiritual LIE...

Lord Please Help Me Break This Down...
James 1:15 SAYS:

¹⁵ Then When Lust Hath Conceived, It Bringeth Forth Sin: And Sin, When It Is Finished, Bringeth Forth Death. .

In Other Words, You Basically Kill Yourself In Your Sin... And The Desire That You Had, Reveals Itself As The Lie It Is And It ONLY Belongs To You...

You're Only Fooling Yourself...

Everything I Went Through Was Unfamiliar,

Unknown,

New,

Strange,

Foreign

And Uncommon To Me

But

REAL.

There Was An Alien Encounter, Anomalous, Which Deviated From What Was "Normal" To Me And It Served Me Something That Was Extraterrestrial In Form, Because It Was Outside The Earth's Atmosphere.

I Could Not "See" It, But I Felt It, I Could Not Hold It, But It Had A "Hold" On Me And After I "Learned" It's Ability To Overtake And Bring Pleasure To Me, I Started Participating In It When It Showed Up.

It Was A Pathway To A Door That Stayed "OPEN"...

Although It Initiated Itself First, My Desire To Be "Satisfied" Entertained It, Because It Was Clean. The Only Problem Was, I Had To Participate In It Even When I Didn't Want To And When I Would "Reject" It, The Force Of It Became "Forceful" And I Tricked Myself Into Believing That

It Was Love Coming From The Person I Desired In A "Foreign" Form...

Lord Help Me...

You See, We Sit In Church And We Have These "Desires" For Men As Single Women And While We're In Church "Worshipping" God In "SPIRIT", We Unbeknown To Ourselves, Enter In Union With Another Spirit And That Spirit Gives Us Just What We Want In Spirit, In The Lie Of Its Existence.

We Are Not Suppose To Be Worshipping God And Thinking About Desire At The Same Time. Every Thought We Have While Worshipping God Should Be To Him, About Him, In Regards To Him. The Spirit World Is So Real And The Bible Says We Are To PULL Down Strongholds...
Desire Can Be A Stronghold.
Want Can Be A Stronghold
And Lust Is Definitely A Stronghold, Whether You Act On It Or Not.
The Mind Can Be A Fierce, Strategic Playground For The Devil And If You're Worshipping And Desiring Something Other Than God, (With Your "Anointed" Self), You Are Definitely In The Playground Of Satan And Every Demonic Force Is Going To "Continuously" Launch An Attack On You.
 Until You "Understand" What It Means To Worship God In "Spirit" And Truth To Do It Indeed, You Will Always Be A "Target" For Deception Especially, When It's Discovered By The *(Shaky)* Person On The "Pulpit" That You Have False Intentions Or Ulterior Motives...

Some Of Us Make Pastor's Prostitutes,
You Know, That's When The Spirit Is High In The Church And Your Lusting, Desiring, Wanting And Your Looking At The Man/Woman Of God That Can "SEE YOU" In The Spirit. Gifts Come Without Repentance And When They Begin To "Prostitute" They're Gifts, And We Start Emptying Out Our Bank Accounts And Emotions And We Get Nothing Back In Return, We Leave The Church. The Truth Is You Should Have Never Played A Game You Could Never Win With Someone That Was Chosen To Pastor.

People Of The Cloth See You In The Spirit A Mile A Way. Basically, You Make Yourself A Target, Until You Get Smart, Which Can Take A Lot Of Going Through. This Book However, Is Designed To **STOP** You In Your Tracks...
God Is A Giver Of Every Good And Perfect Gift.
The Bible Instructs Us To Make Our Request Made Known To God... PERIOD.

The Bible Says In **1 John 4:1-5 King James Version**
4 Beloved, Believe Not Every Spirit, But Try The Spirits Whether They Are Of God:

Please Come On In This Room Yall...

I Am NOT Making This Up...
This Book Is About "Deliverance".
I Am NOT Trying To Entertain You...
Pay "Attention".

Pastor's Know The Word Of God And Some Of Them Will TEST YOU...

The Key Is To **Master The Mastery Of Servitude** So When You Have Any Experience, Bad Or Indifferent, You'll Not Only Be Experienced In It, But You'll Know How To Handle The Experiences, By Using God's Sword To Battle.

You Cannot Win A Battle Against Your Flesh, If You're Participating "Part Time" In The Pleasure Of It, Even In Your Mind!!!

Let's Not Confuse Ourselves, There Is A Battle Going On In Your Mind, In Your Mind, Inside Of Your MIND!!!...

Again, The Bible Says, [4] (For the weapons of our warfare are not carnal, but mighty through God to the pulling down of strong holds;)
(You Have To Learn How To PULL DOWN Strong Holds)...
You Have To Learn How To Cast Down Imaginations And Every High Thing That Exalteth Itself Against The Knowledge Of God, Which Is Sin...

The Knowledge Of God Is Truth And The Truth Is Bigger Than Reality And That Truth Will Set You Free...
And Guess What, I'm Going To Keep Saying This...
Me Telling You The Truth,
Will KEEP ME FREE!!!
LOL...
AND I Am, Laughing!!!

Look, *I Am Not Making This Up...*
Ezekiel 3:18-21King James Version
[18] When I say unto the wicked, Thou shalt surely die; and thou givest him not warning, nor speakest to warn the wicked from his wicked way, to save his life; the same

wicked man shall die in his iniquity; but his blood will I require at thine hand.

^{19} Yet if thou warn the wicked, and he turn not from his wickedness, nor from his wicked way, he shall die in his iniquity; but thou hast delivered thy soul.

The Purpose Of This Book

This Book Is About Exposure AND Deliverance.

There Can Be No Deliverance Without Exposure.

I Did Not Want To Get Into Total Details About "Every" Occurrence, Because I Did Not Think It Was Necessary, But What I Did Think Was Necessary Through The "Directive" Of God Was To Expose Why Some Women Leave The Church, Emotionally Hurt And Financially Ruined, Never To Question What Part They May Have Played In The Ordeal.

I Have Seen Men Strategically, Take Advantage Of Women To The Point The Women Wanted To Commit Suicide. It's Horrible What Goes On In Some Churches, But God Is A Restorer And He Corrects The Errors.

One Thing We Can Count On Is God Taking Vengeance... He Said It Vengeance IS MINE...

I Watched Countless Men Lose EVERYTHING Because Of Their Dark Practices And Although God Avenges Us, He Does Not Want Us To "Glory" In It...

I Had To Discover That, So When God Comes To Your Rescue, Please Restrain Yourself From Saying: "That's What You Get"... You'll Place Yourself Right In The Seat Of Sin And God Judges In Righteousness Which May Not Be Fair To You After The Punishment...

That's Why You Need To Learn THE RULES!!!

Pick Up My Book, "How To Live A Skillful Life – The Shift"...

It Will Definitely Help You, It Helped Me...

Jesus Is Soon To Come And Restoration Is In The House. There Can Be No Restoring If There Isn't Acknowledgment, Exposure, Acceptance And Repentance. We Need To Repair The Breeches And LEARN HOW TO LIVE HOLY...

I Wrote This Book About Sensual Sins In The Temple And I Used What Happened To Me To Introduce It... Everything I Wrote Was True... We Have To Get Our Thoughts In Order And Line Them Up With The Will Of God Or Else They Will Serve To Us Just What We Think And It May Not Be The Way You Expect It To Be...

"Grab A Hold Of Yourself" Another One Of My Books...

God Is Speaking To His People, Wishing That No Man Perish, No Not One...

We Need To Understand Sensual, Innocent Sins, So We Can Stop Participating In Them...

God Is On The Throne And He Is Working Life Out For Me And He's Definetely, Working Life Out For You.

Read Your Bible AND Learn The Rules. Start Trying To Figure Out What Is Acceptable To God And What Is Not. I Always Say, Life Is BIGGER Than Your Reality AND It Is...

The Reality Is, The Wages Of Sin Is Death...

The Reality Is, Only The Righteous Shall See God...

The Reality Is, The Just Shall "Barely", "Barely", Make It In...

Learn What The Reality Is In Christ And Then You'll Be Introduced To The Truth!!!

Enjoy The Scriptures.

AND

MORE Importantly,

LOOK UP THE WORDS I Listed And Read The Scriptures!!!

LOOK UP THE WORDS For A Understanding.

Sometimes You'll Get Things By Writing Them Down And Studying The Meaning. If You Look Up The Words I've Listed, You'll See Things A Little Clearer. I Guarantee It.

Be Informed...

This Is All For You...

Scriptures

JAMES 1
James 1King James Version
1 James, a servant of God and of the Lord Jesus Christ, to the twelve tribes which are scattered abroad, greeting.
2 My brethren, count it all joy when ye fall into divers temptations;
3 Knowing this, that the trying of your faith worketh patience.
4 But let patience have her perfect work, that ye may be perfect and entire, wanting nothing.
5 If any of you lack wisdom, let him ask of God, that giveth to all men liberally, and upbraideth not; and it shall be given him.
6 But let him ask in faith, nothing wavering. For he that wavereth is like a wave of the sea driven with the wind and tossed.
7 For let not that man think that he shall receive any thing of the Lord.
8 A double minded man is unstable in all his ways.
9 Let the brother of low degree rejoice in that he is exalted:
10 But the rich, in that he is made low: because as the flower of the grass he shall pass away.
11 For the sun is no sooner risen with a burning heat, but it withereth the grass, and the flower thereof falleth, and the grace of the fashion of it perisheth: so also shall the rich man fade away in his ways.
12 Blessed is the man that endureth temptation: for when he is tried, he shall receive the crown of life, which the Lord hath promised to them that love him.

¹³ Let no man say when he is tempted, I am tempted of God: for God cannot be tempted with evil, neither tempteth he any man:
¹⁴ But every man is tempted, when he is drawn away of his own lust, and enticed.
¹⁵ Then when lust hath conceived, it bringeth forth sin: and sin, when it is finished, bringeth forth death.
¹⁶ Do not err, my beloved brethren.
¹⁷ Every good gift and every perfect gift is from above, and cometh down from the Father of lights, with whom is no variableness, neither shadow of turning.
¹⁸ Of his own will begat he us with the word of truth, that we should be a kind of firstfruits of his creatures.
¹⁹ Wherefore, my beloved brethren, let every man be swift to hear, slow to speak, slow to wrath:
²⁰ For the wrath of man worketh not the righteousness of God.
²¹ Wherefore lay apart all filthiness and superfluity of naughtiness, and receive with meekness the engrafted word, which is able to save your souls.
²² But be ye doers of the word, and not hearers only, deceiving your own selves.
²³ For if any be a hearer of the word, and not a doer, he is like unto a man beholding his natural face in a glass:
²⁴ For he beholdeth himself, and goeth his way, and straightway forgetteth what manner of man he was.
²⁵ But whoso looketh into the perfect law of liberty, and continueth therein, he being not a forgetful hearer, but a doer of the work, this man shall be blessed in his deed.
²⁶ If any man among you seem to be religious, and bridleth not his tongue, but deceiveth his own heart, this man's religion is vain.

[27] Pure religion and undefiled before God and the Father is this, To visit the fatherless and widows in their affliction, and to keep himself unspotted from the world.

Romans 6 King James Version

6 What shall we say then? Shall we continue in sin, that grace may abound?

2 God forbid. How shall we, that are dead to sin, live any longer therein?

3 Know ye not, that so many of us as were baptized into Jesus Christ were baptized into his death?

4 Therefore we are buried with him by baptism into death: that like as Christ was raised up from the dead by the glory of the Father, even so we also should walk in newness of life.

5 For if we have been planted together in the likeness of his death, we shall be also in the likeness of his resurrection:

6 Knowing this, that our old man is crucified with him, that the body of sin might be destroyed, that henceforth we should not serve sin.

7 For he that is dead is freed from sin.

8 Now if we be dead with Christ, we believe that we shall also live with him:

9 Knowing that Christ being raised from the dead dieth no more; death hath no more dominion over him.

10 For in that he died, he died unto sin once: but in that he liveth, he liveth unto God.

11 Likewise reckon ye also yourselves to be dead indeed unto sin, but alive unto God through Jesus Christ our Lord.

12 Let not sin therefore reign in your mortal body, that ye should obey it in the lusts thereof.

13 Neither yield ye your members as instruments of unrighteousness unto sin: but yield yourselves unto God, as those that are alive from the dead, and your members as instruments of righteousness unto God.

14 For sin shall not have dominion over you: for ye are not under the law, but under grace.

[15] What then? shall we sin, because we are not under the law, but under grace? God forbid.
[16] Know ye not, that to whom ye yield yourselves servants to obey, his servants ye are to whom ye obey; whether of sin unto death, or of obedience unto righteousness?
[17] But God be thanked, that ye were the servants of sin, but ye have obeyed from the heart that form of doctrine which was delivered you.
[18] Being then made free from sin, ye became the servants of righteousness.
[19] I speak after the manner of men because of the infirmity of your flesh: for as ye have yielded your members servants to uncleanness and to iniquity unto iniquity; even so now yield your members servants to righteousness unto holiness.
[20] For when ye were the servants of sin, ye were free from righteousness.
[21] What fruit had ye then in those things whereof ye are now ashamed? for the end of those things is death.
[22] But now being made free from sin, and become servants to God, ye have your fruit unto holiness, and the end everlasting life.
[23] For the wages of sin is death; but the gift of God is eternal life through Jesus Christ our Lord.

Additional Reading

The Number 4 Derives It's Meaning From Creation. On The 4th Day Of Creation Week, God Completed The Material Universe, On This Day God Brought Into Existence Our Sun, The Moon And All The Stars. The Purpose Was Not To Only Give Light, But To Divide The Day From The Night On Earth, Thus Becoming The Demarcation Of TIME!!! They Were Also Made To Be A Type Of Signal That Would Mark Off The Days, Years And Seasons. Interestingly, The Hebrew Word For "Seasons" In Genesis 1:14 Is Moed... Which Literally Translated Is "Appointed" Times... Divine Appointments...

The 4th Of The Ten Commandments Is To Remember And Keep God's Holy Sabbath Day. God Rested In It After Bringing Everything Into Existence.

I Had To Used By God To Write These Books...
I Was Used, Taught, Instructed And Delivered.
It's Incredible.
All The Books Follow Each Other In Order Of A Word For Knowledge, Awareness, Instruction, Correction And Deliverance.
You Have To Grab A Hold Of Yourself In Order To Understand That There's A Conspiracy Against Your Flesh That Happened, Because Of The Treason In The Garden...
Sensual Sins In The Temple Exposes Innocent Sins That You May Not Be Aware Of And Sometimes As A Result Of A Hidden Desire, People Leave The Church... Then Comes How To Live A Skillful Life, Which Comes After Repentance And The Desire To Seek God's Kingdom In Righteousness.

Workbook - WORDS

Below, Is A List Of Words, I Want You To Look Up And Concentrate On Their Absolute

"Defined" Meaning And Definition.

LOOK UP THE WORDS

PLEASE LOOK UP THE WORDS

AND UNDERSTAND THEM

I'll Define One Word So That Your "Pursuit" Is "Aroused".

LOOK At Aroused And You'll See...

My Attempt Is To "AWAKEN" You,

Which Means To Make Someone "Aware" Of Something, Perhaps For The First Time.

Arouse – Evoke Or Awaken (A Feeling, Emotion Or Response). Synonyms: Induce, Prompt, Trigger, Stir Up, Bring Out, Kindle, Fire, Spark, Provoke, Cause, Foster.

Antonyms... Excite Or Provoke (Someone) To Anger Or Strong Emotions... Rouse, Galvanize, Excite, Electrify, Stimulate, Inspire, Move, Fire Up...

Arouse Means To Awaken.

Truth

Worship

Temple

_____

_____

_____

_____

Spiritual

_____

_____

_____

_____

Sensual

_____

_____

_____

_____

Reveal

_____

_____

_____

_____

Sin

Temple

Nonmaterial

_____

_____

_____

_____

Psychological

_____

_____

_____

_____

Esoteric

_____

_____

_____

_____

Extraterrestrial

_____

_____

_____

_____

Foreign

_____

_____

_____

_____

Hedonistic

_____

_____

_____

_____

Sybaritic

_____

_____

_____

_____

Voluptuary

_____

_____

_____

_____

Physical

_____

_____

_____

_____

Carnal

_____

_____

_____

_____

Bodily

_____

_____

_____

_____

Fleshly

_____

_____

_____

_____

Transcendent

_____

_____

_____

_____

Mystic

_____

_____

_____

_____

Intangible

_____

_____

_____

_____

Mental

_____

_____

_____

_____

Pursuit

_____

_____

_____

_____

Pleasure

_____

_____

_____

_____

Creative

_____

_____

_____

_____

Resourceful

_____

_____

_____

_____

Fond

_____

_____

_____

_____

Devote

_____

_____

_____

_____

Pleasure

_____

_____

_____

_____

Self Indulgent

_____

_____

_____

_____

Engage

_____

_____

_____

_____

Activated

_____

_____

_____

_____

Understanding

_____

_____

_____

_____

Opposite

_____

_____

_____

_____

Isolated

_____

_____

_____

_____

Senses

_____

_____

_____

_____

Gratification

_____

_____

_____

_____

Desire

_____

_____

_____

_____

Paradox

_____

_____

_____

_____

Faculties

_____

_____

_____

_____

Sight

_____

_____

_____

_____

Want

_____

_____

_____

_____

Need

_____

_____

_____

_____

Proof

_____

_____

_____

_____

Unwanted

_____

_____

_____

_____

Uncommon

_____

_____

_____

_____

Deliverance

_____

_____

_____

_____

Reveal

_____

_____

_____

_____

Passionless

_____

_____

_____

_____

Coldblooded

_____

_____

_____

_____

Unemotional

_____

_____

_____

_____

Frigid

_____

_____

_____

_____

Journal Your Journey

And

Let The

Journey

Begin

(Journal Your Deliverance)

\-
_____
_____
_____
_____
_____
_____
_____
_____
_____
_____
_____
_____

Published By Books Speak For You Publishing

Specializing In 3, 7 & 21 Day Publishing
Publishing In Over 100 Languages

Printed In The United States

www.Booksspeakforyou.com

1-800-757-0598

1-800-757-0598

Pamela Denise Brown, Author

Creator Of Smart Books And Christian Books For Kids

267-318-8933

Thank You
For Purchasing
This Book
I Hope It Helped You

Pamela Denise Brown

I Released This Book

Christmas Day,

Monday, December 25, 2017

Happy Birthday Jesus

I Dedicate This Book To You

www.ingramcontent.com/pod-product-compliance
Lightning Source LLC
Chambersburg PA
CBHW070920180426
43192CB00038B/2099